A Note to Parents and Teachers

DK READERS is a compelling new reading programme for children, designed in conjunction with leading literacy experts, including Cliff Moon M.Ed., Honorary Fellow of the University of Reading. Cliff Moon has spent many years as a teacher and teacher educator specializing in reading and has written more than 140 books for children and teachers. He reviews regularly for teachers' journals.

Beautiful illustrations and superb full-colour photographs combine with engaging, easy-to-read stories to offer a fresh approach to each subject in the series. Each DK READER is guaranteed to capture a child's interest while developing his or her reading skills, general knowledge, and love of reading.

The four levels of DK READERS are aimed at different reading abilities, enabling you to choose the books that are exactly right for each child:

Level 1 – Beginning to read
Level 2 – Beginning to read alone
Level 3 – Reading alone
Level 4 – Proficient readers

The "normal" age at which a child begins to read can be anywhere from three to eight years old, so these levels are intended only as a general guideline.

No matter which level you select, you can be sure that you are helping children learn to read, then read to learn!

LONDON, NEW YORK, DELHI, PARIS,
MELBOURNE and MUNICH

Project Editors Caroline Bingham
and Penny Smith
Designer Michelle Baxter
Senior Editor Linda Esposito
Managing Art Editor Peter Bailey
Production Josie Alabaster
Jacket Designer Chris Drew
Editorial Consultant
Theresa Greenaway

Reading Consultant
Cliff Moon M.Ed.

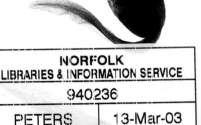

Published in Great Britain by
Dorling Kindersley Limited
80 The Strand, London WC2R 0RL
A Penguin Company

2 4 6 8 10 9 7 5 3

Copyright © 1998 Dorling Kindersley Limited, London

A CIP catalogue record for this book is
available from the British Library.

ISBN 0-7513-5855-X

Colour reproduction by Colourscan, Singapore
Printed and bound in China by L Rex Printing Co., Ltd.

Photography by Paul Bricknell, Jane Burton,
Geoff Dann, Mike Dunning, Neil Fletcher,
Frank Greenaway, Kim Taylor

All images © Dorling Kindersley.
For further information see: www.dkimages.com

see our complete catalogue at
www.dk.com

READERS

BEGINNING TO READ 1

Tale of a Tadpole

Written by Karen Wallace

A Dorling Kindersley Book

The tale of a tadpole
begins in a pond.
Mother frog lays her eggs
next to a lily pad.

jelly

Each tiny egg
is wrapped
in clear jelly.

5

Inside the jelly
the eggs grow into tadpoles.
They wriggle like worms.

They push through the jelly
and swim in the water.

They breathe through gills,
just like fishes.

gills

Many other animals
live in the pond.

There are goldfish and
sticklebacks and
great diving beetles.

They chase the young tadpoles.

A stickleback feels hungry.
His mouth is wide open.

The little grey tadpoles
wriggle their tails ...

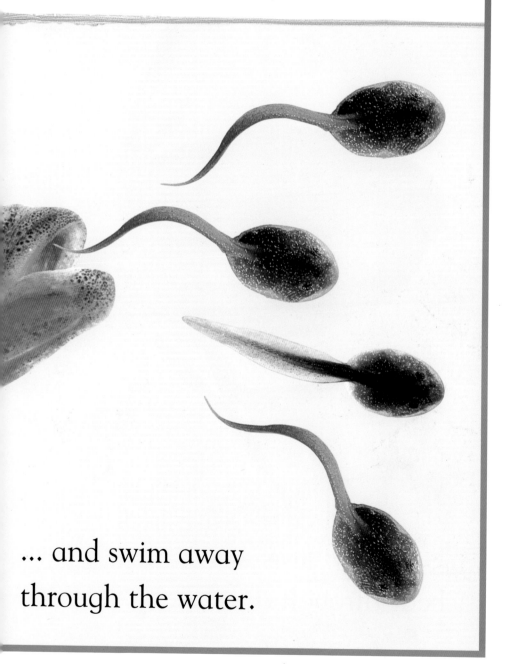

... and swim away
through the water.

A great diving beetle
also feels hungry.

His hairy back legs
beat through the water.

The tadpoles escape
and hide in the weed.

Soon a tadpole
grows legs
with tiny webbed toes.

webbed
toes

Webbed toes are like flippers.
They help the small tadpole
push through the water.

The tadpole grows arms
with long skinny fingers.

fingers

He nibbles on plants and gobbles green pondweed.

Half tadpole, half frog,
he rests in the sunshine.

His tail is shrinking.

tail

It gets smaller and smaller.

The new little frog
sits on a lily pad.

His legs are quite strong now.
He can breathe through his nostrils.
His skin is dotted
with tiny gold spots.

nostril

Frogs must keep their skins slimy.
He hops back in the pond.
He swims for a while
then climbs on to a log.

Another frog climbs up and
sits down beside him.

Now fully grown,
he dives through the water.

He's not afraid of the stickleback.

He swims past the beetle.

In the pond
he watches and waits.
What can he see
with his round beady eye?

eye

A fly lands
above him.
He creeps
closer and closer.

But a big frog jumps up.
It snatches the fly
with its long, sticky tongue.

tongue

The frog
misses his meal.
He'll be quicker
next time.

The golden-skinned frog
chases a dragonfly.
It lands on a lily pad.
Under the lily pad are
hundreds of frogs' eggs.

Inside each egg
a tadpole is growing.
Each tadpole will grow
into a golden-skinned frog.

Picture Word List

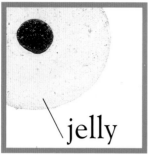

jelly

page 5

tail

page 18

gills

page 7

nostril

page 21

webbed
toes

page 14

eye

page 26

fingers

page 16

tongue

page 28